SWAMI VIVEKANANDA

Swami Vivekananda was born on 12th January, 1863 in Calcutta (Kolkata). His name was Narendranath. His father Shri Vishwanath Dutt was a renowned lawyer in Calcutta High Court. His mother Smt. Bhuvaneshwari Devi was a pious woman, a worshipper of Lord Shiva.

Narendranath was extremely intelligent and quite naughty as a child. He played his pranks on friends and given a chance, he didn't spare even his teachers.

His house followed a regular routine of prayers and other religious activities. Being a devout woman, Bhuvaneshwari Devi liked to listen to Puranas, Ramayana, Mahabharata etc. Priests used to read out these epics for her. The religious and intellectual atmosphere that prevailed in the family had a very positive effect on little Narendranath. The notions of religiosity, noble character and adhyatama were deeply ingrained in his little mind.

Little Narendranath was influenced by the devout character of his parents and the surroundings. He developed a quest for knowledge, existence of God and other divine mysteries right from childhood. Sometimes the parents and teachers were dumbfounded by his queries.

The parents doted on their child prodigy and brought him up

with all the comforts. A tutor taught him at home. At the age of 5 years, little Narendra started studying sincerely. Apart from the studies he was also interested in the religious activities. He made it sure to attend them, whether in the house or in the neighbourhood.

A very interesting incident happened to him as a child. There was a huge garden in the premises of his mansion. One day he sat there meditating with his friends. A black snake came near them and positioned itself in a tray kept in front of Lord Shiva's idol. Children, sensing the movement of snake, opened their eyes and ran away. They called his mother to the garden. She was shocked at what she saw there. Snake was sitting upright in front of the child and he had no idea of what was happening around. Instead of shouting Bhuvaneshwari Devi prayed to Lord Shiva to spare his son. After a while snake went away without harming the child. On being woken up from his meditation, when Narendranath was told about the whole episode he remained calm. This was the most unexpected reaction from a five-year old child.

Right from his childhood, Narendranath thought and acted like grown ups. He calmly analysed the situation around and then took his own decisions.

Small things disturbed little Narendranath whereas another child might not even notice them. Once Khan Saheb, a client of his father, came to his house. His father had gone out of station so Khan Saheb stayed on. He was very fond of Narendranath. The pranks and intelligence of this child never failed to impress him. Narendranath came running to Khan Saheb and both of them started playing. Suddenly Narendranath saw the bag of Khan

Saheb and asked, "Khan Chacha, what is there in this bag?" "It has very tasty sweets," replied Khan Saheb. The name of sweets brought a twinkle in his eyes and very innocently he said, "I love sweets."

Khan Saheb was put in a dilemma. He could not refuse Narendranath but at the same time the child's mother would not let him accept anything from a Muslim. Khan Saheb could not muster courage either to refuse the child or to overlook his mother's religious feelings. Finally, affection prevailed over everything else and Khan Saheb gave some sweets to Narendranath. He took the sweets to his mother. She slapped him in her anger. Narendranath could not understand why he was slapped. The other day his mother had scolded him for coming near to the sweeperess of the house. He wanted to know why all this was happening.

One day Narendranath's mother had arranged a katha of Lord Hanuman. The child was listening to the stories with great interest. While narrating the stories of Lord Hanuman, the priest told that Lord Hanuman had conquered death by emulating the virtues of bachelorhood. He lived forever and dwelled in the garden of banana trees.

On hearing this, Narendranath wanted to meet Lord Hanuman. It struck him that they too have a garden of banana trees so why not look for Lord Hanuman there. He got up and went to the garden. He sat beneath a banana tree for hours waiting for Lord Hanuman to turn up but all his efforts turned futile. He went home and cried in front of the idols of Lord Rama and Sita.

That was not the end of it. Next day while going for regular rides in his chariot, he asked the charioteer, "Uncle, where can I meet Lord Hanuman?" Charioteer had no appropriate answer, so he kept quiet. When Narendranath repeated his question, the charioteer replied, "It is very difficult to find Hanumanji. You will have to adhere to the virtues of bachelorhood all your life." The child replied, "Fine, then I'll never get married and follow the dictums of bachelorhood all my life". On returning home, he told his mother about his pledge. She was overwhelmed with joy at his innocence.

After completing his primary education, Narendranath took admission in Metropolitan Institute, Calcutta (Kolkata). His friend circle started growing gradually. He had a very hectic schedule—going to school, playing games after coming home, learning music, riding horses, meditating and actively participating in other activities. He could not sit idle at one place.

When Narendranath was 14 years old, he once fell very ill. His father was posted in Raipur, Madhya Pradesh. He called Narendra to Raipur after knowing about his illness.

Raipur was a getaway to natural beauty for Narendranath. He was intellectually stimulated with the nature's abundance found in the mountains, and thick jungles full of unexplored green vegetation. All these gave birth to a strange energy in him. Narendra regained his health during the 2 years he spent in Raipur. He glowed with health and energy.

Narendra returned to Calcutta (Kolkata) after 2 years. His studies were disrupted due to his absence for so long. But he got re-admission after completing his school education with good results.

At the age of 18 years, Narendranath joined the Presidency College, Calcutta. His health deteriorated again and he had to discontinue his studies. He lost his one year due to ill health. As he got well, he took admission in General Assembly College.

Narendranath was very interested in philosophy. He was interested in the philosophy of life and divinity right from childhood. His quest for knowledge increased day by day. His interest developed into such a commitment that while studying literature and philosophy no one could disturb his concentration. He studied all the western philosophies in his college life.

Narendranath had a very melodious voice. He participated in all the intellectual assemblies and gatherings held in the city. He mesmerized the people present there with his songs and bhajans.

Once there was a festival organised at Narendranath's neighbour, Surendranath's place. Saint Ramakrishna Paramhansa was to arrive for the discourse. The ceremony started with Narendranath's song. Everyone including Ramakrishna Paramhansa were mesmerized with his voice. The saint called for Narendranath after the song. Saint Ramakrishna blessed him, as he bowed in front of him. The touch of the saint filled him with a divine light. Ramakrishna Paramhansa invited Narendranath to Dakshineshwar for further discussions.

In the summer vacation, while he decided to go to Dakshineshwar, his parents put the proposal of marriage before him. He declined to marry. He was not born to lead life like an ordinary man. He had come to this world to abolish the prevalent misdeeds—superstitions, illiteracy, evil practices in the name of

religion and caste etc. He was born to reform the society.

Narendranath reached Dakshineshwar with some of his friends. His mind was full of contradictions and questions. Shri Ramakrishna Paramhansa was delighted to see him. He said, "You are not an ordinary soul. You have a great spirit inside. What you are, I recognised you that very day."

Narendranath returned home after meeting Swamiji and pondered for long about that visit. Finally, he concluded that he would put his problems to him. If the saint could provide answers and introduce him to the real truth, he could accept the saint as his guru, teacher and devote his life to him.

Brahmo Samaj had been founded by that time. Its reformist spirit had highly impressed Narendranath. He sometimes participated in the functions of the Brahmo Samaj.

Narendranath met several saints and preachers in search of the answers that he desperately wanted, but none he found capable enough. Finally, he went to Swami Ramakrishna Paramhansa and asked him, "Sir, have you seen God?" Swamiji softly replied, "Yes son, I have and if you too want to see God, I can make it possible. But for that you'll have to leave everything and come to me."

Narendra was delighted with the thought of meeting God. He, henceforth, dedicated his life in the service of Swami Ramakrishna Dev.

One evening, Swami Ramakrishna was preaching to Narendra who was sitting before him. Suddenly he got up and touched Narendra's shoulder with his right foot. His touch washed away all the queries out of Narendra's mind. He felt as if

everything around him had sublimed into a divine light, and only he was there in the universe. Then Swamiji put his right hand on Narendra's heart and everything became normal. Narendranath accepted Ramakrishna Paramhansa as a divine teacher. His life got a new turn. Swami Ramakrishna's affection was also showered on Narendra. Later one day Narendra took the oath of leading the life of an ascetic with love and blessings of Swami Ramakrishna Paramhansa.

With the beginning of his ascetic life, Narendra got a new name from his Guru Swami Ramakrishna Paramhansa—Swami Vivekananda. After that the Guru imparted all his knowledge and powers to Swami Vivekananda, so that he could devote himself in the service of mankind and make the nation proud of him.

His preaching to Swami Vivekananda was, "An ascetic's life is meant for social service without an ambition or personal goals in mind. One who only thinks of his salvation, is very greedy. People around you are bound by the chords of pain and suffering. An ascetic's aim in life is to liberate them. If you want to see God, then serve mankind, the human face of the Almighty."

Shri Ramakrishna Paramhansa took 'Mahasamadhi' in August 1886. After that, Swami Vivekananda shifted to Brahnagar Muth. Here he studied a number of books on various religions and philosophy. Swami Vivekananda led other disciples of Shri Ramakrishna Paramhansa on the path shown by the latter. Prayers, discussions and study of various religious books, meditation and chanting went on uninterrupted. Swami Vivekananda was the soul of all the ascetics there. His orders were the orders of the Guru. Swami Vivekananda visited all the

holy shrines in UP and Bihar when he was all of 27 years only. He met many intellectuals, philosophers and religious teachers on his way. He came across various saints and holy men. The only question that he wanted to know was how can the poverty and hunger-stricken people of this country be relieved from their misery. People were impressed with his intellect and concern for the underprivileged. Many joined him in his mission and gradually his fan following increased.

Swami Vivekananda visited Kashi, Prayag, Mathura, Vrindavan etc. On his route, he somehow felt that there is no paucity of devotion in the people towards their religion, its just that social norms hamper the free flow of their participation.

An All-Religion Assembly was to be held on 11th Sept. 1893 in Chicago, U.S.A. Representatives of various religions were to participate in it from all over the world. India too sent its representatives to the assembly. Swami Vivekananda was also one of them, courtesy some of his enthusiastic disciples.

In the conference, everyone got a chance to speak. Swami Vivekananda patiently waited for his turn. As his name was announced, he reached the stage. Saffron clothes, sharp eyes and a poised demeanour — people were astonished to see a queer looking speaker. When Swami Vivekananda started his deliberations on the Hindu Dharma, people were dumbfounded with his logic and elaboration. While introducing the fundamental Dharma of India he said, "The Dharma which I represent is the eternal Hindu Dharma. Its basis is the well-being of the human kind. It is an all encompassing Dharma which includes all the other religions of the world."

Swamiji's speech left such an impression on the people he became the talk of the town. After spending sometime in Chicago, he moved to New York. When he spoke on Rajayog (Governance) and Gyanayog (Meditation), people all over Asia, Europe and Arab countries were impressed with Swamiji's knowledge. They invited him to their countries and took an oath to spread Swamiji's message and to serve him all their lives.

After his successful trip abroad, he was received in India with great enthusiasm. He started the Ramakrishna Mission on 1st May, 1887.

On 4th July, 1903, this great saint of India left for his heavenly abode.

□□□